Lothian
Edited by Annabel Cook

 Young**Writers**

First published in Great Britain in 2007 by:
Young Writers
Remus House
Coltsfoot Drive
Peterborough
PE2 9JX
Telephone: 01733 890066
Website: www.youngwriters.co.uk

SB ISBN 978-1 84602 991 2

Foreword

Young Writers was established in 1991 and has been passionately devoted to the promotion of reading and writing in children and young adults ever since. The quest continues today. Young Writers remains as committed to the nurturing of poetic and literary talent as ever.

This year's Young Writers competition has proven as vibrant and dynamic as ever and we are delighted to present a showcase of the best poetry from across the UK and in some cases overseas. Each poem has been selected from a wealth of Little Laureates entries before ultimately being published in this, our sixteenth primary school poetry series.

Once again, we have been supremely impressed by the overall quality of the entries we have received. The imagination, energy and creativity which has gone into each young writer's entry made choosing the poems a challenging and often difficult but ultimately hugely rewarding task - the general high standard of the work submitted ensured this opportunity to bring their poetry to a larger appreciative audience.

We sincerely hope you are pleased with this final collection and that you will enjoy Little Laureates Lothian for many years to come.

Contents

Angus Hastie (7)	48
Ellis Fleming (7)	49
Rhiannon Kane (7)	49
Jonathan Pryde (7)	49
Paige Williams (7)	50

Paradykes Primary School

Christopher Petrie (10)	50
Amy Clark (10)	51
Hamish Rutherford (10)	51
Nathaniel Lock	52
Kara Casey (10)	52
Holly Cochrane (10)	53
Matthew Paris (10)	53
Nicole White (10)	54
Dannielle Clarke (10)	54
Peter Chater (10)	55
Kinza Mahmood (10)	55
Danielle Wheeler (10)	56
Ryan Goodall (9)	56
Jamie-Lee Baigan (10)	57
Amy Young (10)	57
Josh Witherspoon (10)	58
Liam Mackay (9)	58
Holly Ritchie (10)	59
Daniel Mitchell (9)	59
John Gallagher (9)	60
Eilwen Lyon (9)	60
Greg Cowan (9)	60
Kelly McIntosh (9)	61
Aaron McIntosh (9)	61
Calum Gray (9)	61
Danielle Watson (9)	62
Jamie Ralston (9)	62
Callum Buntin (9)	62
Scott Stenhouse (9)	63
Sarah Walker (9)	63
Scott Montgomery (9)	63
Logan Hercus (9)	64
Daniel Cherrie (9)	64
Kirsty Macbeath (9)	64

St Mary's RC Primary School, Edinburgh

Tom Brooke (8)	65
Sophie Lynn (9)	65
Declan Logan (9)	65
Flora Hughes (8)	66
Oliver Smith (8)	66
Charlotte Lazarowicz (8)	67
Marisha Worsnop (8)	67
Stephanie McAdam (8)	68
Tallulah McCowan Hill (8)	68

St Peter's Primary School, Edinburgh

Lloyd Anderson (12)	69
Cameron Pullar (11)	69
Stephanie Cremona (8)	70
Saoirse Robertson (9)	70
Lucy Malloy (8)	71
Adele Pacitti (7)	71
Sam Jefferson (8)	72
Sarah Denholm (11)	72
Niamh Jarvis (8)	73
Shaun Newman (11)	73
Lucie Keenan (8)	74
Eithne FitzGerald (11)	74
Joanna Thomson (7)	75
Ciara Sawey (7)	75
Lishan Qian (9)	76
Beth Howard (9)	76
Martina Rossi (9)	77
Francesca Faichney (9)	77
Emily Turnbull (8)	78
Lewis Gormley (8)	78
Moreen Randall (11)	79
Leon Siebke Ballin (11)	79
Ronan Mullan (11)	80
James Monan (8)	80
Sophie Darbyshire (10)	81
Cathy Chiduku (8)	81
Chloe Bruce-Gardyne (10)	82
Rose Johnstone (11)	82
Anna McNairney (10)	83

Sophie McKenzie (10)	83
Erin Mackinnon (10)	84
Lisa Wilson (10)	85
Tom Donovan (7)	85
Patrick Faichney (11)	86
Kirsty Galbraith (10)	86
Sarah O'Brien (11)	87
Simon Wilson (7)	87
Nicole Ojok (11)	88
Lucy Cairns (11)	88
Fraser Johnston (11)	89
Carrie Malloy (11)	89
Rhona Lilley (9)	90
Marc Fleming (9)	90
Andrei Vitaliev (9)	91
Finlay MacKenzie (9)	91
Aidan Mooney (11)	92
Kirsty Lilley (11)	92
Katie Jefferson (11)	93
Jacqueline Flynn (8)	93
Silvie Walker (11)	94
Lucy Sharpe (11)	94
Catherine Donovan (11)	95
Molly McCloy (11)	95
Amy O'Sullivan-Robertson (8)	96
Sarah Wilson (8)	96
Ciara Keenan (8)	96
Flora Bruce-Gardyne (8)	97

Stoneyburn Primary School

Skye Sutherland (9)	97
James Bleakley (10)	97
Francesca McGraw (9)	98
Katie Abbott (9)	98
Jamie Green (9)	99
Summar Blair (9)	99

The Poems

Silent Peace

Peace is baby-blue like a clear sky
on a beautiful summer's day.

It sounds like silence
and time to think things over.

It smells like sweet red roses
and the welcoming scent of home.

It looks like wild horses galloping past
without a care in the world.

It feels like a newborn baby's hand
squeezing your fingers for comfort.

It tastes like sweet ripe strawberries and cream
with the juice dribbling down my chin.

Peace reminds me of a calm still lake
with no ripples on a warm summer's day.

Emma Egan (10)
Bellsquarry Primary School

Fun

Fun is orange like a huge orange sun.
It sounds like oranges rolling about in the giant fruit bowl.
It smells like sweet melon squirting.
It looks like children playing and having fun.
It feels like sweet honey.
It tastes like sweet lemons
And it reminds me of very fun things to do.

Ross Carruthers (10)
Bellsquarry Primary School

Kindness

Kindness is pink like a blossoming flower
in springtime.

It sounds like the birds
singing and kisses being given.

It smells like the grassy meadows
with the newborn lambs running about.

It looks like the leaves dropping off the trees
that are growing gracefully.

It feels like a big love heart
hugging me all the time.

It tastes like my favourite food
on a hot summer's day.

Kindness reminds me of people
who love me.

Helen Traill (11)
Bellsquarry Primary School

Happiness

Happiness is light blue like the lovely blue sky in the summer.
It sounds like a nice cold summer breeze.
It smells like a light blue summer day.
It looks like a little girl with light blue clothes and a happy family.
It feels like everyone loves me.
It tastes like a bright summer's day.
Happiness reminds me of the best day ever.

Ashley McAdam (10)
Bellsquarry Primary School

Loneliness

Loneliness is white like a blank canvas
just waiting to be used.

It sounds like a hollow tree
in a long-forgotten land.

It smells like burning rubber
in a field of golden corn.

It looks like a small boat
lost on the horizon.

It feels like
all hope is lost.

It tastes like bitter sauce
or flat Coke.

Loneliness reminds me of despair,
blundering around in the dark.

Megan O'Neill (10)
Bellsquarry Primary School

Oh Happiness

Happiness is orange like a gorgeous, sunny, warm day.
It sounds like laughter and happy joy.
It smells like a cold ice cream on a warm sunny day.
It looks like fireworks in the dark black sky.
It feels like a big, hot, warm sun.
It tastes like a juicy ripe orange.
Happiness reminds me of kind happy people
                sitting next to a warm orange fire.

Monica Roscilli (10)
Bellsquarry Primary School

Loneliness

Loneliness is dark blue
like a night at stormy sea.

It sounds like a silent earthquake
waiting to happen.

It smells like you are rotting
with no one to care about you.

It looks like a nightmare
when awake.

It feels like you are an invisible man
walking right through people.

It tastes like sour strawberries
from 1901.

It reminds me of a toy
with no owner.

Euan Donald (10)
Bellsquarry Primary School

Happiness Forever

Happiness is orange like a ball of joyful flames.
It sounds like children playing on a warm summer's day.
It smells like sweet oranges and fresh fruit in a bowl.
It looks like tropical fish and water fresh and pure.
It feels like silk as it flows through your fingers.
It tastes like sweets, chocolate and cream.
Happiness reminds me of new flowers in spring
And the chirp of happy birds.

Jessica Harvey (10)
Bellsquarry Primary School

Happiness

Happiness is blue like the summer's sky
swaying in the air like a peaceful butterfly.

It sounds like the world is so peaceful
and nothing will disturb you.

It smells like your favourite food
flying through the air.

It looks like a DB9
and you are driving to the Earth's limits.

It feels like the world is standing still
and you have all the time in the world.

It tastes like a giant sweet
and chocolately eclair.

Happiness reminds me of the big,
nice, sweet and happy world.

Jonathan White (10)
Bellsquarry Primary School

Happiness

Happiness is pink like a heart full of joy.
It sounds like fireworks setting off in the blue, calm sky.
It smells like cotton candy swirling in the machine.
It looks like a pink morning sky.
It feels like a breeze of wind.
It tastes like strawberry jam.
Happiness reminds me of people being happy.

Shannon-Lee Cross (10)
Bellsquarry Primary School

Fun

Fun is orange
like a sweet and juicy tangerine.
It sounds like children
laughing all day.
It smells like marshmallows and doughnuts
at the carnival stall.
It looks like the biggest, the longest
and the fastest roller coaster in the world.
It feels like candyfloss
sitting on a stick.
It tastes like sugar
in the Coca-Cola.
It reminds me of Christmas
that happens once a year.

Iain Henderson (10)
Bellsquarry Primary School

Anger

Anger is orange like a fearsome raging fire destroying a town.
It sounds like the screams of dying people.
It smells like smoke, thick and poisonous.
Anger looks like blood lying on freshly fallen snow.
It feels like cold dull metal, plain and bland.
It tastes like Mexican spices that are so hot.
Anger reminds me of rage and destruction that is all around us.

Jake Thomas (10)
Bellsquarry Primary School

Happiness

Happiness reminds me of butterflies
hovering over my head on a warm day in the sunlight.
Happiness feels like rabbits
jumping in a field of flowers.
Happiness tastes like a big red apple
crunching in your mouth.
Happiness smells like a burning candle
with love in the steam.
Happiness looks like children
playing together in a park on a sunny day.
Happiness sounds like a bird
singing the sweetest song you have ever heard.
Happiness is as gold as a pot
at the end of the rainbow.

Chloe Blyth (9)
Bellsquarry Primary School

It's A Sad World

Sadness is blue like a frozen sun in the middle of winter.
Sadness sounds like water running down a great mountain.
Sadness smells like a leftover quarry.
Sadness looks like a shivering seal under a deep blue icy sea.
Sadness feels like a heart-thumping earthquake
                              that's only just happened.
Sadness tastes like a sour, rotten blueberry.
Sadness reminds me of when no one would play with me

And that's a sad world!

Andrew Hutchinson (10)
Bellsquarry Primary School

Happiness

Happiness is the light blue sunshine at the open beach
shining on top of you.
Happiness feels like a soft squishy marshmallow
with different flavours inside.
It tastes like creamy ice cream
waiting for you to eat it up.
It smells like hot spicy fajitas
with a hot smell in the cooker.
Happiness reminds me of my grandma
when I was wee.
It looks like a picture of my grandma
with my grandad on the sofa.
It sounds like a chirping
in the morning sunshine.

Calum McLean (9)
Bellsquarry Primary School

The Erupting Volcano

Anger is red like the lava erupting from the volcano.
It sounds like thunder and lightning coming down from the sky.
It smells like something burning in the distance.
It looks like fire surrounding you in a jungle.
It feels like the ground is shaking underneath you.
It tastes like steaming hot chocolate in the early morning.
Anger reminds me of my sister and I fighting.

Jenna Moir (10)
Bellsquarry Primary School

Happiness

Happiness is yellow, like sweet sticky caramel,
taking over your mouth.

Happiness smells like a sweet-smelling buttercup,
tickling your nose.

The sound of happiness is like little blue tits,
chirping in a green-leaved tree.

Happiness looks like a newly grown rose bush,
that's glistening in the hot summer sun.

The feeling of happiness is like a soft fluffy sheepskin
rubbing against your cheek.

Happiness reminds me of the trickling sound
of a clear, pure water stream.

Emily Smith (9)
Bellsquarry Primary School

Silver Dream

Joy is silver like an Aston Martin DB5 shining in the sun.
It sounds like the laughter of children playing and having fun.
It smells like apple pie with runny cream.
It looks like a tropical forest, growing with plants and trees.
It feels like marshmallows smothered in chocolate sauce.
It tastes like ice cream and pancakes tasting so sweet.
It reminds me of Christmas when I got my Xbox 360.

Nikolas Hogarth (10)
Bellsquarry Primary School

Anger Is . . .

Anger is the colour red, a deep volcanic red
that you would hear and feel in a volcano.

It reminds me of a volcano about to erupt,
little bubbles and fizzes, sparks already flying out.

Anger looks like a broken heart,
crumbling into splintering pieces.

What remains of the heart is turning black,
as black as smoke.

Screaming like a baby is what anger sounds like;
a lion's roar that echoes through the deep cave.

Anger smells like an egg, a rotten egg, weeks, months,
possibly years old now, frying in a frying pan.

Bubbling inside, fizzing, that is what anger feels like.
Steam coming from my ears faster than a train
with extra steam puffing out the engine, about to explode.

Anger is the taste of a rotten egg that is years old.
The one with green inside, as green as grass in summer
and the shell as brown as a conker.

Emma Richardson (9)
Bellsquarry Primary School

Pink Is Amusing

Amusement is pink like the candyfloss at the fair.
It sounds like laughter echoing in a tunnel.
It smells like pancakes smothered in a rich chocolate sauce.
It looks like a mountain of presents at Christmas.
It feels like your birthday you've been waiting forever for.
It tastes like a birthday cake with divine chocolate sponge.
Amusement reminds me of birds, free to roam
                              in the warm summer sky.

Kirsty Lee (10)
Bellsquarry Primary School

Happiness

Happiness is yellow like the glowing sun,
shining brightly on the countryside.

The feel of happiness is like the softest pillow
to make you always dream good dreams.

It looks like trees in spring
showing their beautiful blossoms to all the world.

Happiness reminds me of spending time with my family
on a hot sandy beach.

The sound of happiness is like cats purring and miaowing
to comfort each other.

Tasting happiness is like marshmallows on a stick
next to a burning campfire.

Happiness smells like the sweet-smelling scent
of beautiful flowers.

Hannah Robinson (9)
Bellsquarry Primary School

Anger Is . . .

Anger is the colour red like a red frog.
It sounds like a bird screeching forever.
It tastes like a solid meatball that came from an artificial workshop.
It reminds me of death, red and unforgiving.
It smells like shoes from the 1800s
And it looks like a raging whirlpool sucking up all in its path.
It feels horrible like razor-sharp spikes of steel.

David Musil (9)
Bellsquarry Primary School

Happiness

Happiness is as yellow as the golden sun
on a hot summer's day.

It smells like a lovely warm sponge cake
that has just come out of the oven.

Happiness reminds me of crisp snowflakes
falling onto the cold wet snow.

It tastes like a soft marshmallow
that melts in your mouth.

Happiness sounds like cheerful birds
chirping on an oak tree.

It looks like oozing chocolate
spurting out of a chocolate fountain.

Happiness feels like spongy play dough
squishing in your hands.

Brodie Walker (9)
Bellsquarry Primary School

Sadness

The colour of sadness is blue like the ocean waves.
It feels like the soft feather from the eagle dropping
                                      on the burning sand.
It feels like the most fantastical stream's water.
What it reminds me of is the tears from the ugly duckling.
Your sadness looks like the boy who lost his teddy bear.
The smell of sadness is like the rain after five days.
Sadness tastes like a sour lemon freshly cut in half.

Harry Miles
Bellsquarry Primary School

Jealousy Is . . .

Jealousy is green like a big, enormous slimy monster
creeping up a hill.

It reminds you of a volcano
about to erupt on the massive hillside.

Sometimes it feels like a piece of charcoal
chipped and sharp, just about to go into a fire.

It tastes like a rotten apple,
sour like you could ever imagine.

Sometimes it smells like a pickle,
very strong, like a rotten carrot.

Jealousy looks like a tiger catching its prey
in the warm jungle with the grasslands.

Jealousy sounds like the roar of a tiger
running to catch her cub.

Zoë Baxter (9)
Bellsquarry Primary School

Love

Love is the colour of a red, red rose.
It has the sound of a little baby bird as it tweets.
Love looks like a couple hand in hand.
It has the smell of a lovely sweet.
Love has the taste of melted chocolate on your tongue.
It feels like a warm cosy rug.
Love reminds me of the romantic Valentine's Day.

Sophie Howieson (9)
Bellsquarry Primary School

Anger With The Devil

Anger is as red as the Devil underground, 500ft
with a razor-sharp pitchfork too.

It feels like a bull's razor-sharp horns
who needs his meat for tea.

The taste of it is like the juiciest apple ever,
but it's haunted.

Sounds like screaming because some person got so angry,
punched the screamer - dead.

Anger smells like the nasty red smelly peppers
my dad puts in his red-hot curries.

The feel of anger is as red as red-hot crackling flames
from the fire.

Anger reminds me of the time my face
turned to the colour bright red.

Andrew Reid (9)
Bellsquarry Primary School

The Red Anger

Anger looks like a fierce lion about to attack.
It sounds like a bubbling volcano about to erupt.
Anger feels like a big black deathtrap
                about to pull you down a red hole.
It tastes like a rotten egg in a sandwich
                left over for weeks and weeks.
It reminds me of a really horrible day in autumn.
Anger smells like rotten cheese with out-of-date eggs.
Anger is the colour of red.

James Jenner (9)
Bellsquarry Primary School

Darkness

Darkness is as black as coal
that has been sitting there for years.

Darkness feels like you are falling down a never-ending hole
that has nothing but darkness at the bottom.

The smell of darkness is like a rotting apple growing on a tree
that is dying from the lack of sunlight.

The sound of darkness is like always being alone,
no one seems to talk, the only sound is the wind
whooshing past your ears.

It looks like a midnight sky
with not a shining star or moon.

It tastes like frozen food grating at your teeth
leaving shreds upon your lips.

Darkness reminds me of a night with a full moon
that is haunted by witches and werewolves.

Lara Prigmore (9)
Bellsquarry Primary School

Sadness Is Like . . .

Sadness reminds you of the Grim Reaper brushing past your spine.
Sadness is the colour of a dull grey cloud that is hanging
over your head.
It looks like a dead bird just lying there in the cool air.
It tastes like a bit of apple pie that is five days out of date.
Sadness sounds like the hard pitter-pattering on the roof.
It feels like the sharpest needle that's clinging on to my skin.
Sadness looks like a river of tears colliding together
to make an ocean of them.

Andrew Paterson (9)
Bellsquarry Primary School

Anger

Anger is the colour of red
like boiling hot lava spilling out of a volcano.

Anger feels like you're a steam train
going very fast.

It tastes like spicy chilli peppers
with even more hot sauce covering them.

Anger smells like wood burning
in the flames of fire.

It reminds you of the most embarrassing
moment in your life.

Anger sounds like someone
shouting really loud at you.

Bailey Blyth (9)
Bellsquarry Primary School

Love Is Like . . .

The colour of love is like a red, red rose.
Love reminds me of looking in the sky of twinkling stars.
It feels like a silky smooth scarf.
Love tastes like melting chocolate in your mouth.
It sounds like the gentle tinkling of keys.
Love looks like crystal-clear water.
It smells like a big bundle of flowers.

Georgia Hogarth (9)
Bellsquarry Primary School

Sadness Is . . .

Sadness tastes like a rotten banana
with brown bruises.

Sadness feels like you're all alone
in the big dark world.

Sadness looks like a classroom
with one child alone and the others
laughing at him.

Sadness sounds like people
shouting at you for no reason.

Sadness smells like chemical gases
in the air.

Sadness reminds me of losing
the people I love very much.

Hannah McClennon (9)
Bellsquarry Primary School

Happiness

Happiness is the colour of a bright blue butterfly.
It looks like smiles appearing on a child's face.
Happiness feels like your head resting on a soft pillow.
It smells like honey dribbling down the trunk of a tree.
Happiness tastes like jelly wiggling down your throat.
It reminds me of happy children playing in a park.

Sam Reid (9)
Bellsquarry Primary School

Fear Is Darkness

Fear is black like the dark night sky
at midnight.

It reminds you of a dark room
covered with black and nowhere to go.

It smells like someone's cursing breath
when no one is there.

Fear sounds like someone yelling,
yelling, 'He's coming to get you!'

It feels like a pale hand
reaching to grab you from behind.

It looks like a huge lava monster
stopping you from breathing in.

Fear tastes like a revolting apple
forcing its way down your throat.

Euan Roach (9)
Bellsquarry Primary School

Love

Love is the colour of red hearts.
Love looks like mum and son holding hands.
Love smells like tulips growing in the garden.
Love tastes like the sweetest of sweets in the whole universe.
Love sounds like air floating in the sky.
Love feels like soft, soft play dough.

Henna Mohammed (9)
Bellsquarry Primary School

Anger Is Like . . .

Anger is like a big dark hole about to erupt.
It reminds me of a wrecking tornado destroying the village.
It feels like a big dark hole waiting to cover you up.
It tastes like a bitter, sour apple covered in gloopy glue
waiting to go in your mouth.
It smells like a rotten apple in the dumpster.
It looks like a red devil about to attack you!
It sounds like a bull about to charge at you!
The colour is like a damp colour, black, boring!

Bannewel Karley (9)
Bellsquarry Primary School

Hunger

Hunger is like a brown plate with nothing on it.
It sounds like a rumbling stomach, starving for food.
It smells like rotten goo you need to eat.
Hunger tastes like eggs left out for years.
Hunger feels like the wind telling you there is no food.
It reminds you of a horrible mother who has not fed you in years.
Hunger looks like a desert going on forever.

Duncan Roach (9)
Bellsquarry Primary School

Jealousy

Jealousy is the colour of a green, ugly monster with red eyes.
It tastes like the most sour, juicy apple ever.
Sometimes it reminds me of an orange volcano about to erupt.
Jealousy looks like a lump of red strawberry jam.
It sounds like a tornado raging over the houses.
Jealousy feels like a spiky green caterpillar.

Charlotte Gallagher (9)
Bellsquarry Primary School

What Fear Is Like

Fear reminds me of ghosts waving about like sheets.
Fear feels like you're falling down a black hole.
Fear tastes like loads of prickly spines clinging to your throat.
Fear smells like rotten vegetables bubbling in a cauldron.
Fear looks like red spots jumping on you.
Fear sounds like freaky noises happening in the night.
Fear's colour is green and orange mixed together.

Connor Smith (9)
Bellsquarry Primary School

Jealousy Is . . .

Jealousy is as purple as the violet flower.
The smell of jealousy is like burning brown cake in the oven.
It tastes like cold, bubbly, fizzy juice fizzing in your mouth.
Jealousy sounds like the ocean waves crashing against big rocks.
It reminds me of a big, green slimy monster coming out of the ocean.
Jealousy feels like touching a very spiky, prickly cactus.

Ella McFarlane (9)
Bellsquarry Primary School

Happiness

Happiness feels like a rainbow with every colour.
It sounds like blue whales swishing in the sea.
The taste is like white chocolate.
Happiness smells like lavender and camomile.
It reminds me of a snowman dancing on ice.

Georgi Murray (9)
Bellsquarry Primary School

Anger Is . . .

Anger looks like a rumbling volcano on the verge of eruption.
It tastes like a huge jar of the spiciest spice ever made.
Anger reminds me of me and my sister fighting.
It is red like hot bubbling lava.
Anger sounds like a fire burning the pitch-black coal.
It feels like my body is swelling up.
Anger smells of burning sweat dripping from my head.

Matthew Hallesy (9)
Bellsquarry Primary School

When I Was Ten

Last year when I was ten
I saw my tree come down
The tree was as big as a monster
I was as shocked as a block
I thought I was in a dream
I was as sad as a crab
But that was last year, I'm 11 now.

Graham Reid (11)
Borthwick & Temple Primary Schools

Last Year When I Was 8

Last year when I was 8,
I saw a hedgehog lying still,
I tasted chicken that was like an over-cooked rabbit,
I stopped believing in Santa,
It made me feel so happy,
But that was last year, I'm 9 now.

Steven Lennie (9)
Borthwick & Temple Primary Schools

What's A Hawk?

What's a zebra?
It's black and white
Both day and night

What's a giraffe?
Tall and brown
But does not frown

What's a penguin?
Black and white
But doesn't fly like a kite.

But what's a hawk?
Just a soaring hawk.

Cameron Mackie (10)
Borthwick & Temple Primary Schools

What Is . . .

What is a mum?
She's helpful and handy,
Even if her name is Mandy.
What is a dad?
He's big and scary,
We call him Mary.
What is a brother?
He's annoying and loud,
He makes Mum proud.
What is a dog?
A dog is simply just a dog.

Kirsty Scott (10)
Borthwick & Temple Primary Schools

Preposition Poem

On a spotty mat
there was a brown cat
chasing its tail

In the jungle
there was a swinging monkey
eating a banana

In a zoo
there was a fierce lion
growling in its bed.

Demi-Leigh Anderson (8)
Echline Primary School

Mars

M ars is a big red planet
A huge, ginormous planet
R ed, orange and yellow
S lowly turning around.

Ross Doyle (8)
Echline Primary School

Butterfly Up In The Sky

Up in the sky.
A pretty butterfly flying so high
Trying to find the way home.

Jenna Beveridge (8)
Echline Primary School

My Bed

My bed is a comfy cloud floating across the sky.
It is a colourful and bright butterfly fluttering by.

My bed is a warm and toasty hot summer's day.
My bed is a hideaway den where I sit and play.

My bed is a net which tucks me in tight.
It is the warm sun shining bright.

My bed is a purple heaven in a lilac dream.
It is a waterfall with a long running stream.

Emma Scott (10)
Echline Primary School

Wings

(Inspired by 'If I Had Wings' by Pie Corbett)

If I had wings I would touch the candyfloss clouds
If I had wings I would taste them too
If I had wings I would hear aeroplanes going past
If I had wings I would smell the fresh air
If I had wings I would see and feel the hot sun on my face!

Fraser Merritt (8)
Echline Primary School

The Rain

The rain is a beating drum on my window.
It is a waterfall running down the drains.
The puddles are swimming pools in my garden.
The rain is an ice-cold needle stinging my face.
It is a grey blanket covering my house.

Siobhan Gunn (10)
Echline Primary School

Solar System

S aturn getting closer to me
O rbiting the Earth
L unar Rover rumbles over rough surfaces
A tmosphere getting further away
R ockets shoot by like lightning

S un not far away
Y ipes, sun getting very hot
S pacesuit can't resist the heat
T riumphant stars pass by
E normous planets pass
M eteorites almost hit me!

Craig Potter (8)
Echline Primary School

Creepy-Crawly

Under a damp
log
a big spider
crawling
away
under some
leaves.

Megan Porteous
Echline Primary School

Pluto

P leading for sunlight
L onely at the end
U nder no circumstance
T his could be the end
O n the little planet Pluto.

Stuart Robertson
Echline Primary School

Wings

(Inspired by 'If I Had Wings' by Pie Corbett)

If I had wings I would touch the flying birds
If I had wings I would taste the candyfloss clouds
If I had wings I would hear the people down below
If I had wings I would smell the pizza from the chip shop
If I had wings I would see my house in the distance.

Rhys Laird (8)
Echline Primary School

Bowling

As I approached the green for bowling
I noticed that the gardener had finished mowing.
I walked up the garden path
And smelt the clean cut of grass.

The sun was warm, skies were blue
The nod was given, it was my cue.
I took out the bowls to start to play
I knew I was going to enjoy my day.

Quietness, except the sound of bowls clicking
It was tense, we could hear the clock ticking.
I let out a yell so I could tell
'Yes!' I had won, my day was done.

Pierre Mitchell (11)
Flora Stevenson Primary School

Rubbish

Recycle, recycle
You can even recycle your old bicycle

Smelly wellies
Watch what to do with them on your sister's telly

The landfill sites are really stinky
With dirty old toys and old Tinky Winkys
They're full of waste
With a dreadful taste
And when the wind blows
You'll hold your nose

So . . .

Take your old tins to the recycling bins
All your old clothes, to a charity shop, they go
Wash your old toys that are very mucky
And pass them to those who are not so lucky

Make a New Year's resolution
And try not to cause so much pollution.

Ella Duffy (10)
Flora Stevenson Primary School

Under The Sea

Swirling pools of blue glistening water,
Tropical fish swimming by, orange, purple, blue and green too.
The smell of saltwater fills the air like vinegar on salted crisps.
Giant sharks like huge worms with fins circle the poor
                              helpless fish like dogs chasing cats.
The big round sun, a ball of fire, reflecting in the water.
Clumps of coral seem like giant clumps of candyfloss.
The scuba gear is strapped tight to my body.
Ripples from my hands make the water bubbly and wavy.

Catriona Nicolson (11)
Flora Stevenson Primary School

The Football Match

The gates open and the fans
Rush to their seats like a stampede of zebras
Being chased by a leopard.

The queue for the tickets
Is filling up like an hourglass.

After the two teams warm up and the game starts
The whole stadium lights up
And you wouldn't know if the world blew up
Because the songs and chants are so loud.

The whistle goes
Piercing through the stadium,
It's a penalty!
There is a tense silence.
All you can see is a sea of heads.
The player takes the run up
And the crowd cheer
Like a whole pack of lions roaring loudly.

The whistle goes for half-time
And the fans quickly go for a pizza and a pie
Before they disappear like a shadow
In a dark alleyway.

The second half is played.
The winning fans are cheering
Like they have won already.
The losing fans are leaving early.

The final whistle and the crowds leave
Cheering as if they've won the World Cup.

Ross Hunter (11)
Flora Stevenson Primary School

Stormy Weather

The first signs of a storm are slight.
A few drops of rain fall from the sky.
The clouds gather.
Big grey ones that block out the sun completely.
The sky turns black.
There is a rumbling sound coming from above.
Thunder and lightning.
Hail.
The clouds open up!
People run for cover.
Storm ends.
Sun shines.
The only remains of the storm are puddles of water.
And of course, the rainbow.

Kim Gray (9)
Flora Stevenson Primary School

Summer Is Beautiful

Summer brings buzzy bees
Summer opens flowers
Summer brings the sun
Summer takes you to the beach
Summer brings you on a holiday
Summer is beautiful.

Emily Ross (7)
Flora Stevenson Primary School

What I Found Under My Bed

What did I find under my bed?
Did I find a famous artist?
Did I find his art?
Did I find a princess?
Did I find her prince?
Did I find Charlotte?
Did I find her web?
Did I find an alien?
Did I find its spaceship?
Did I find a girl?
Did she have a curl?
No, I found an old dusty photo album with pictures of . . .
Me, in my mummy's tummy.
From the first time I smiled
To the last time I saw my dad.

Mary McIntosh (8)
Flora Stevenson Primary School

A Little Living Planet

A little living planet
Just about to die,
Not enough recycling,
The world's about to die,
Not enough people choose to recycle.
The ice caps are melting too quickly,
Come on, there must be some way,
We will die if the trees die,
So come on, recycle your rubbish!

Keir Logan (7)
Flora Stevenson Primary School

Can You Hear It?

Can you hear it?
Can you hear the birds in the tree?
Can you hear the rain tapping on the windowpane?
Can you hear the cricket in the garden hopping along?
Can't you hear it?

Flora Reid (7)
Flora Stevenson Primary School

Hot Sand

Sunny days you go to the beach
You feel all the warmth of that sun up in the high sky
You can feel the sun on your feet
It feels as if you're walking on clouds
You can feel that the sun is right underneath you.

Hansine Marshall (7)
Flora Stevenson Primary School

Hearing

Can't you hear the sound of music
Of . . . blossom trees blowing with their lovely green leaves
Of . . . the birds singing with their kind sweet voice
Of . . . the gentle lapping from the lake
Of . . . me, touching the sound of snow.

Ellen Francis (8)
Flora Stevenson Primary School

Look? Look?

Where are the ducks in the pond?
Where have the birds gone?
Where have the squirrels gone?
Where have the fish gone?
When I went to the park
I never saw any animals at all
Where have they gone?
Can you help me please?

Purum Singh (8)
Flora Stevenson Primary School

Winter Park

Under the trees
A fox ready to catch a rabbit.
By the bandstand
A frozen statue.
On the hill
Children having a snow fight.
At the swings
Two children flying.

Nicolas de Silva (7)
Flora Stevenson Primary School

Listen

Listen to the trees swishing
Listen to the water splashing
Fish swimming
Dogs running
Leaves falling
Listen to the butterflies flapping
Listen to the bees buzzing.

Zoe Laxton (7)
Flora Stevenson Primary School

At The Seaside

In the blue sky
Seagulls are soaring.
On the hot sand
Adults sunbathe.
Out in the sea
Boats are sailing.
At the shore
A child jumping over a wave.

Samira Ali (7)
Flora Stevenson Primary School

Xmas Morning

Xmas morning, the start of the day
Wake up, wake up I say
There are presents to open
And new games to play
Santa has been with his sleigh
And hey!
Have a happy Christmas I say.

Sophia Woodside (8)
Flora Stevenson Primary School

The Bike

The bike is quick
The bike is slick
It gets me to school in a tick.
But now I walk to school each day
It takes me ages, it's such a long way.

Lucie Duffy (7)
Flora Stevenson Primary School

The Emotions

Happy, sad, angry, furious
We are the emotions can you see?
We live in your head or sometimes in your heart
We come out when you smile or when you part.
When you are angry we jump around in your head
And sometimes we stay there until you go to bed.

Jamie Bingham (8)
Flora Stevenson Primary School

Scotland

The lochs are deep.
The mountains sleep.
The rive's run fast.
The salmon leap.
The eagle soars on wings so wide.
Fishing boats leave with changing tide.

The thistle, it jags our sore feet.
It's time for home and haggis and neeps.

The rain, it pours and soaks us through.
The wind it blows and turns us blue.
Scotland is where I was born.
Forever Scotland I belong.

Anna Escott (9)
King's Park Primary School

Scotland's Heart

(Inspired by 'Magic Box' by Kit Wright)

I will put into the box . . .
the autumn race for the fallen conkers,
the River Tay shining in the evening sun,
the happiness of children playing in the snow.

I will put into the box . . .
the Scottish saltire flying on Scots buildings,
the Hampden roar when Scotland score,
the Flying Scotsman steaming on its tracks.

I will put into the box . . .
the taste of mince and tatties after a long day out,
the joy of a little taster of Irn-Bru at the café,
the whole haggis for the family on Burns Night.
Truly this is Scotland's heart.

Andrew Fowler (10)
King's Park Primary School

Scotland

There is a monster called Nessie,
She is very messy,
People come from miles around,
But she is nowhere to be found.

Haggis, neeps and tatties,
Is a tasty meal for fatties,
Wash it down with whisky booze,
Then you'll have a lovely snooze.

Soaring high up in the sky,
You can see a golden eagle fly,
If you're lucky you might see,
A golden eagle by the sea.

Murray Legge (9)
King's Park Primary School

Scotland The Best

Scotland is ma country
Scotland is ma hame
The only thing that's disappointing
Is a' the wind an' rain.

The scenery is awesome
As I walk doon the street
Oor national team are nae saer guid.
They often mak me greit.

Scotland is famous for a' sorts o' things
From golf tae the Heelan' fling
From Edinburgh Castle tae Nessie
An' the midgies that often sting.

I like tae read oor Wullie
The Broons are guid fun too
There's lots tae dae in Scotland
Like a trip tae Edinburgh Zoo.

I hope ye enjoyed ma poem
I'm awa' tae hae ma dinner
But if I dinnae eat ma grub
I'll end up gettin' thinner.

Daniel Hall   (10)
King's Park Primary School

Scotland

S o, you want to know about Scotland,
C ould have sun, rain, thunder, lightning,
O r even could have a rainbow,
T o know about Scotland, you need to live in it,
L ovely scenes with the Pentlands and the sun,
A nimals like golden eagles, red deer and adders,
N obody really knows about Scotland if you think about it,
D o you know about my home now?

Duncan McQueen   (9)
King's Park Primary School

Imagine My Country

Imagine mist-covered mountains and deer roaming the glen
Where great battles were fought by many brave men.

Imagine small villages by lochs, small boats on their shore
And many a tale steeped in folklore
Well Scotland has this and much, much more.

Imagine cities and towns with castles of old
Each with a story to be told
Imagine good weather all the year round
I am sorry to say, this cannot be found.

Oh well, never mind
Wherever you go the people are kind.

Imagine a clear mountain stream as it rushes by
And the eagle as it soars high in the sky
A bird so proud and glad to be free
Living in Scotland, just like me.

Shannon Hawkins (9)
King's Park Primary School

Scotland

S cottish scenery is superb, the Scots would call it braw,
C elebrating Burns Day is good fun, haggis and neeps and aw.
O ther things to celebrate - the Scots won many a battle,
T histles helped wi' one of them but noo they're eaten by cattle.
L och's the word that we use, English call 'em lake,
A n' summit lives inside yin, make nae mistake.
N essie is so famous, the tourists all believe,
D id ye ken when they get here they dinnae want to leave?

Charlotte Holland (9)
King's Park Primary School

The Wee Hing

This is a tale of a funny wee'hing
Who really, really 'hinks he cin sing
He has a furry wee tail 'n' a wee white leg
Watch if he nips ye it stings like a cleg
He lives in the Highlands 'n' has a pink spotty beak
He sings when the sun sets, aw! it's more like a shriek!
He's loud 'n' noisy, so high-pitched and shrill
It's a gid jobe he bides at the tope of a hill
He's two red fiery eyeballs inside his plump head
They stared at me while a wis tucked up in ma bed
A grabbed him in a deep dark pail
I had to be very hasty
Cos he looked exceedingly tasty.

William Hutchison (9)
King's Park Primary School

Scotland

In Scotland there are lots of things to do
Loads of wildlife in the zoo

At Edinburgh Castle the wind can chill
But the view is worth the climb up the hill

At one o'clock you'll have some fun
As the tourists jump at the sound of the gun

Edinburgh is a fantastic city
Please visit us, if you don't it's a pity.

Stephanie Birrell (9)
King's Park Primary School

Scotland The Brave

Scotland is so good
With the grass so green,
Scotland is the best,
England were so mean,
At the Battle of Bannockburn
Scotland found its son,
A man called Wallace,
Oh! what have they done?
England wanted our land,
Scotland had its man.

Darren Fleming (9)
King's Park Primary School

Edinburgh

Edinburgh is a city.
It's always very busy.
It made me feel so dizzy,
when I went shopping for my bear Izzy.
Edinburgh is a great Scottish city.

Megan Connolly (9)
King's Park Primary School

Scotland

S cotland flags swaying silently in the wind.
C old rain dripping on our heads.
O wls flying low at night.
T horny thistles in the green grass.
L ovely flowers in groups of six.
A nimals running about in the woods.
N oises of nature all around the air.
D ifferent rivers all throughout Scotland.

Claire Graham (9)
King's Park Primary School

Scotland

Scotland makes me think of prickly thistles.
Prickly thistles makes me think of colourful tartan.
Colourful tartan makes me think of Scottish dancing.
Scottish dancing makes me think of musical bagpipes.
Musical bagpipes makes me think of the blue and white saltire.
The blue and white saltire makes me think of Scotland.

Scotland makes me think of glorious Scottish food.
Glorious Scottish food makes me think of thirling whisky.
Twirling whisky makes me think of leaping salmon.
Leaping salmon makes me think of sizzling haggis.
Sizzling haggis makes me think of steaming mince and tatties.
Steaming mince and tatties makes me think of Scotland.

Scotland makes me think of hazardous history.
Hazardous history makes me think of Scottish heroes.
Scottish heroes makes me think of William Wallace.
William Wallace makes me think of freedom fights.
Freedom fights makes me think of tragic Culloden.
Tragic Culloden makes me think of Scotland.

Scotland makes me think of sight-seeing places.
Sight-seeing places makes me think of breath-taking Edinburgh.
Breath-taking Edinburgh makes me think of the majestic Highlands.
The majestic Highlands makes me think of eye-catching Stirling.
Eye-catching Stirling makes me think of monstrous Inverness.
Monstrous Inverness makes me think of Scotland.

Natsumi Honjigawa (9)
King's Park Primary School

Fresh Air

While walking through the hills and glens
The splendour of the countryside is here
Deep breaths of pure fresh air
It has to be Scotland for me.

Emma Thomson (9)
King's Park Primary School

A Scottish Sorrow

(Dedicated to Sir Robert the Bruce)

I have seen the bloody battles fought
I have seen my people so distraught
I have felt a thistle's spike
It's not as painful as an Englishman's strike.

As I fought in those dark glens
Against Edward's soldiers from above the Thames
And as the English have no excuse
They turn to face Sir Robert the Bruce.

I have seen the innocent killed
But still I know it is God's will
And as we charge with tartan and sword
I look forward to freedom which is our reward.

As I fought in those dark glens
Against Edward's soldiers from above the Thames
And as the English have no excuse
They turn to face Sir Robert the Bruce.

And as there is no fear of English knives
We may carry on to live our lives
Now war is over and we have no sorrowful tears
For Sir Robert has helped to defeat our fears.

David Kerr
King's Park Primary School

Scotland

Scotland makes me think of shaggy Highland cows.
Shaggy Highland cows make me think of haggis, neeps and tatties.
Haggis, neeps and tatties make me think of fast-flowing rivers.
Fast-flowing rivers make me think of clear blue lochs.
Clear blue lochs make me think of spiny-backed Nessie.
Spiny-backed Nessie makes me think of the St Andrew's flag.
The St Andrew's flag makes me think of Scotland.

Erin Murray (9)
King's Park Primary School

Scotland

Scotland has a lot of good sights,
to go and see when it's bright.

If you want to bag a Munro
just put on your things and go.

Come and see the Highland cattle
or where Wallace and Bruce did battle.

Scotland has a lot of good sights
to go and see when it's bright.

Hannah Cameron (9)
King's Park Primary School

Scotland

S cottish saltires flapping to and fro
C astle windows so shiny that they glow
O utings across the hillside, such a long walk
T ourists come from everywhere to look, point and talk
L ochs where you can see big Nessie
A nimals and farms are very messy
N ettles and thistles crowd around our feet
D ull weather like rain and fog and sleet.

Katy Wynne (9)
King's Park Primary School

Scotland

There once was a lassie called Tess.
She lived up beside Loch Ness.
Where we like our lattes.
She loved mince and tatties
And her beautiful red tartan dress.

Abby Clelland (9)
King's Park Primary School

Scotland Makes Me Think Of . . .

Scotland makes me think of faithful Greyfriars Bobby
Faithful Greyfriars Bobby makes me think of adventurous castles
Adventures castles makes me think of tragic Mary Queen of Scots
Tragic Mary Queen of Scots makes me think of
majestic Holyrood Palace
Majestic Holyrood Palace makes me think of the windswept saltire
The windswept saltire makes me think of extraordinary Scotland.

Elena Connarty (9)
King's Park Primary School

Hope

If hope was a colour it would be pure white.
If hope was a sound it would be a hummingbird's song.
If hope was a taste it would be like a cold refreshing glass of milk.
If hope was a smell it would be lavender in full bloom.
If hope was a creature it would be a pegasus flying free.
If hope was a feeling it would be soft and silky like my housecoat.
If I could see hope it would be a world full of peace and harmony.
Hope lives in our heart and in the hearts of everyone
around the world.

Becky Preston (11)
Knightsridge Primary School

My Best Friend Hannah

Hannah is like a nice, comfy, soft sofa.
She is like a peaceful, quiet and calm evening.
If she was a fruit she would be a soft juicy strawberry.
If she was a type of weather she would be beautiful hot sunshine.
She is like a cosy, cuddly white rabbit.

Shona Whillans (8)
Longniddry Primary School

Journey For Water, Journey For Life

Journey for water, journey for life,
Baking in the hot African sun,
Jackals howl and tigers prowl
As I go plodding by,
Landmines and bombs under my feet,
Warthogs squeal and cry,
Waterhole - dusty and old -
As I go staggering by,
Monkeys chatter in the trees
As I've got very weak knees,
Waterhole polluted,
Muddy water evaporating fast!
The search goes on,
At last fresh, cool, clean water
To save my family!
As I go triumphantly by!

Alasdair Semple (7)
Longniddry Primary School

Anger

Anger is like a roaring, scary volcano.
It is like a roaring fire.
Anger smells like burning toast.
It sounds like a roaring devil behind me.
Anger reminds me of crazy electric guitars.
It looks like burning bonfires.
It feels like a huge thunderstorm.

Callum Russell (8)
Longniddry Primary School

Animal Families

My mum is like a koala bear
because she is cuddly.

My dad is like an elephant
because he is strong.

My granny is like a monkey
because she likes bananas.

My grandad is like a tiger
because he hunts in the garden.

But I am like a dolphin
because I am such a good swimmer.

Lizzie Clelland (8)
Longniddry Primary School

Sarah

S tar at maths.
A lways happy and joyful.
R eally, really cool.
A very smart chap.
H elpful and kind.

Sarah Brogan (8)
Longniddry Primary School

Andrew

A lways a good friend.
N ever ever mean.
D efinitely works hard.
R eally likes running.
E yes are brown.
W ell-mannered boy.

Andrew Conlin (7)
Longniddry Primary School

Journey For Water, Journey For Life!

I am on a journey for my family's life.
Bombs exploding when I don't know.
Tigers growling and scaring the living daylights out of me.
All wells empty.
Walking for eleven hours until I finally get some water.
Hooray!
I have saved my family's life,
Thanks to the water!

Rachel Thomson (7)
Longniddry Primary School

Rage

Rage is like the colour red, an angry devil.
It feels like green, slimy Brussels sprouts.
It sounds like a hurricane sucking people up.
It looks like a massive tarantula sucking people's blood.
Rage smells like a raging bull with smoke coming out of its ears.
It reminds me of my angry dad!

Ross Stevenson (7)
Longniddry Primary School

My Best Friend Shona

Shona is like a beautiful, sweet-smelling vase of roses.
She is like a calm, peaceful evening by the fireplace.
If she was a fruit she would be a sweet strawberry.
I like Shona because she is like a sunny beach.
She is like a beautiful chestnut pony with a beautiful soft, furry coat.

Isla Semple (7)
Longniddry Primary School

Michael

M ichael likes to run.
 I ntelligent and good friend.
C lever and cheerful boy.
H elpful pupil and fast racer.
A lways smiling.
E specially loves drawing.
L aughs a lot.

Michael Ferguson (7)
Longniddry Primary School

Playtime

Basia is chasing the boys
Ally is eating his snack
Callum scores a goal
Lizzie is kissing Callum
Rhiannon is crying
It's playtime again!

Olly Bradley (7)
Longniddry Primary School

My Sister

My sister is like a big bouncy bed.
She is wide awake after lunch.
A big juicy pear she is.
Rainy, stormy weather she is like.
She is a little furry koala.

Rachel Wilson (7)
Longniddry Primary School

The Senses

I like the taste of pizza
sizzling on my tongue.

I like the smell of flowers'
perfume at my nose.

I like the feel of rabbit fur
tickling on my hand.

I like the sound of barking
loudly in my ears.

I like the look of rabbits
jumping in the zoo.

Lindsay White (7)
Longniddry Primary School

When I Grow Up . . .

When I grow up . . .
I'm going to be a ballet dancer.
I will dance around
I will dance for the Queen
I will dance to anyone
I love it! I love it I do
I will do nothing else
Nothing, nothing else.

Jack Algeo (7)
Longniddry Primary School

Angus

A lways friendly.
N ever in a bad mood.
G reat fun to be around.
U sually helpful.
S miles a lot.

Angus Hastie (7)
Longniddry Primary School

Animal Families

My mum is like a cat
because she looks like one.

My dad is like a baboon
because he stinks.

My sister is like a zebra
because she always wears stripes.

But I am like a puppy dog
because I'm smart.

Ellis Fleming (7)
Longniddry Primary School

Love

Love is pink like a pink butterfly.
It sounds like a kiss from the wind.
Love tastes like pink lipstick.
It looks like people cuddling each other.
Love feels like a kiss.
It smells like perfume.
Love reminds me of my mum and dad.

Rhiannon Kane (7)
Longniddry Primary School

Rage

Rage is like a boiling volcano about to blow!
It is like red, blasting, bubbling lava.
It sounds like a bolt of lightning striking a building
With fire spreading all over.
It looks like dead people lying on the ground.
It feels like watery blood running down the river.
It reminds me of a burning building,
Smoke rising into the sky.

Jonathan Pryde (7)
Longniddry Primary School

Paige

P ersonal writing is her favourite.
A lways caring.
I s a good friend.
G reat at maths.
E verybody likes her.

Paige Williams (7)
Longniddry Primary School

Night

Night to me is a scary place to be,
I often feel my spine shivering,
Hearing strange noises,
Full of coldness,
No light,
Just night.

Night to me is a scary place to be,
Objects below my window,
Seeing unusual shapes,
No movement anywhere,
I had a poor sight,
Just night.

Night to me is a scary place to be,
The wind is blowing rapidly,
Lying on my bed,
There is not a sound,
I could never get a fright,
Just night.

Christopher Petrie (10)
Paradykes Primary School

Dark Night

Lying still in my bed,
Darkness is all around,
Very scared lying there,
Silence.
Silence.
There was not a sound.

Lying still in my bed,
So scared I can't speak,
Watching shadows on the wall,
Petrified.
Petrified.
There was not a peep.

Lying still in my bed,
Clouds separated from the moon,
Looking at my small clock,
Hoping.
Hoping
That it would be daytime soon.

Amy Clark (10)
Paradykes Primary School

Night Of Evil

Mist looming silently over the quay,
Darkness gliding through the deserted flats,
Thrashing trees making me scared,
Brutal bats biting cats,
Mist looming silently over the quay,
Nestling in my bed are the devils,
Feasting ghouls on the hills,
The giant hunter revels,
Mist looming silently over the quay,
Dust flying into the big dark forest,
Lying on the ground are ghosts.

Hamish Rutherford (10)
Paradykes Primary School

Night

To me night is full of horrid shapes,
Of goblins and bloodsucking bats,
Of people screeching
And monsters staring,
Of rats rustling
And witches with their skinny black cats.

To me night is full of horrid shapes,
Of sticks snapping,
Of creatures stirring
And vampires sucking blood,
Of ghosts howling
And werewolves lapping.

To me night is full of horrible shapes,
It sends a chill down my back
And scares me out of my skin,
I dream of horrible creatures,
When objects go crack.

Nathaniel Lock
Paradykes Primary School

Night Of The Ghosts

The ghostly moon hovering in the sky
Attempting to attack rats,
Dark walls closing in,
Alarming shadows and black cats.

The ghostly moon hovering in the sky
Sending a message of danger,
Fearful goblins under the bed,
Trying to attack a stranger.

The ghostly moon hovering in the sky
Glowing with impending doom,
Darkness creeping over me,
But I know dawn will come soon.

Kara Casey (10)
Paradykes Primary School

Night

To me night is peaceful and calm,
The small bushes whistle in the wind,
The twinkling sky shines down on the sea,
Everyone in their beds sweetly sleeping,
I can see the long grass softly swaying,
The moon makes silhouettes of the trees.

To me night is peaceful and calm,
I can see the animals searching for food,
The owls are hooting on branches of trees,
I can see them in the air lurking for food,
The mountains standing still
While the trees are blowing in the breeze.

Holly Cochrane (10)
Paradykes Primary School

Night

To me night is full of peaceful things
Like moonlit trees swaying softly,
And children snug up in their beds,
Owls silently hunting for food,
The cats slowly moving past,
And stars gleaming in the sky.

To me night is full of peaceful things
Like the moon just sitting in the sky,
And foxes quickly running by,
The river flowing through the hills,
The foxes scurrying into their dens,
And golden leaves gently flying by.

Matthew Paris (10)
Paradykes Primary School

A Peaceful Night

On a peaceful night I often see,
The moonlit trees swaying softly,
The stars glistening in the sky,
The night birds swooping past,
And children lying snug in their beds
And seeing leaves gently fly by.

On a peaceful night I often see,
The cats silently strolling past,
The windmill turning round and round,
The wheat in the fields drifting side to side,
And the owls looking out for prey
And the flower heads travelling across the ground.

On a peaceful night I often see,
The moon lighting up the pond,
The rabbits hopping down their holes,
The adults sitting by the fire,
And the faint mountains standing tall
And creeping badgers, foxes and moles.

Nicole White (10)
Paradykes Primary School

The Silvery Night

I like night when it is peaceful not spooky,
The silvery moon looks down on the calm river,
Children all snuggle in their beds,
Cats stroll around the houses,
Lights on,
All quiet.

I like night when there is no sound of the wind,
I am cosy in my bed looking down on the town,
Reading my book all snuggled
In my duvet all soft and cosy,
Book down,
Lights off.

Dannielle Clarke (10)
Paradykes Primary School

Peaceful Night

The night is a peaceful room which I love,
A spotless moon
And a wind so light,
The gleaming stars
And the moon at such a height,
And the sky that looks so restful.

The night is a peaceful room which I love,
The smell of a roasting fire,
And the soft wind that I hear
Of trees rustling,
And not a tear
Of the river wearing away.

The night is a peaceful room which I love,
Of the great silence,
And animals sleeping,
Of shooting stars,
And no phones bleeping,
Until the sun appears.

Peter Chater (10)
Paradykes Primary School

Sparkling Night

The night is a magnificent new place,
A starry sky is very glittery and peaceful,
The peaceful sight to me
Is a great place to be,
The leaves are sparkling
Like many diamonds.

The night is quiet and shimmering,
The cats are playing and pouncing,
The moon is shining bright,
And the stars are a sparkling sight,
The trees are twinkling,
And the leaves are soundless.

Kinza Mahmood (10)
Paradykes Primary School

Peaceful Night

When I look out my window at night I see . . .
The magnificent moonlit sky shining down at me,
Owls quietly looking for their prey,
The silvery river floating calmly,
I can see leaves falling gently,
The children snug in their beds peacefully.

When I look out my window at night I see . . .
The moon shining down against the trees,
The swans drinking the water from the flowing river,
The newborn chicks snug in their nests,
The smell of frothy hot chocolate coming through my bedroom door,
And the scent of marshmallows coming in my window
                              from the glowing fire outside.

When I look out my window at night I see . . .
Still silhouettes brushing against the trees,
Badgers and moles quietly digging up holes,
Rats silently creeping past my house,
Rabbits hopping gleefully,
The peaceful night, you will see.

Danielle Wheeler (10)
Paradykes Primary School

I Have A Dog In Me

Retrieving quickly
Viciously barking
Peacefully jumping
Ferociously eating
Everybody looking at me
Everybody knows me
I feel special.

Ryan Goodall (9)
Paradykes Primary School

Silent Night

No noise, nothing, except the fire crackling,
The moon is sleeping quietly,
Shooting star moving quickly,
The stars are moving slowly,
Warmness I feel.

No noise, nothing, except the cat snoring,
Smooth pink cover keeping me warm,
Clock clicking slowly,
Shooting stars zooming quickly,
Happiness I feel.

No noise, nothing, except the bird squeaking,
Lying in the living room,
Shadows moving slowly,
I sleep quietly,
Quietness I feel.

Jamie-Lee Baigan (10)
Paradykes Primary School

To Me Night Is . . .

To me night is a weary sky
Of ghouls, monsters and bats,
Of eerie winds rustling
And black scary cats,
The murky, thick clouds cover up the moonlit sky
Of freezing fog and silence creeping through the night.

To me night is black, weary sky.
My heart's pounding with fear,
Silhouettes gleaming,
Poison floating through the air,
People screaming,
Smells like blood overflowing the night.

Amy Young (10)
Paradykes Primary School

Night Poem

Darkness is for evil,
With ghosts dancing round glowing fires
While werewolves howl loudly
Enjoying fresh human flesh,
And the moon moves round the Earth
Looking for evil.

Darkness is for evil,
With bright shining eyes
In the field of witches and warlocks
Eating rat meals,
Owls hooting for their prey, with me
Watching playing with my wheels.

Darkness is for evil,
With zombies knocking on the window
And witches under the floor,
Then all I hear next is
A shake on the floor,
Spiders coming under the bed,
All I can do next is get out my bed.

Josh Witherspoon (10)
Paradykes Primary School

I Have A Baboon In Me

I have a baboon in me
Climbing quickly
Joyfully jumping
Peacefully sleeping
Eating quietly
Everybody knows him
Everybody likes him
He feels happy.

Liam Mackay (9)
Paradykes Primary School

Scary Night

An ominous owl scanning,
Rivers smashing together angrily,
Slinking near comes a cat,
Scurrying ghastly rat,
Frightened, frightened.

An ominous owl scanning,
The wind roaring in my face strongly,
Shining across the land,
Floating beastly hand,
Horrified, horrified.

An ominous owl scanning,
At night the bushes rustling loudly,
Treating ghosts above my head,
Terrifying wolves under my bed,
Terrified, terrified.

Holly Ritchie (10)
Paradykes Primary School

I Have A Monkey In Me

I have a monkey in me
Climbing quickly
Happily swinging
Noisily talking
Eating silently
Everybody looking at him.
Nearly everybody knows him.
He is very excited.

Daniel Mitchell (9)
Paradykes Primary School

I Have A Monkey In Me

I have a monkey in me
Climbing joyfully
Loudly jumping
Growling ferociously
Nobody knows him
He does not care
Because he has his friends around him.

John Gallagher (9)
Paradykes Primary School

I Have A Cheetah In Me

Running eagerly
Angrily sleeping
Peacefully eating
Growling horribly
Everybody looking at her
Everybody running away
She feels so proud.

Eilwen Lyon (9)
Paradykes Primary School

I Have A Monkey In Me

I have a monkey in me
Swinging peacefully
Terribly cheeky
Loudly sleeping
Eating excitedly
Everybody likes him
And he's happy.

Greg Cowan (9)
Paradykes Primary School

I Have A Monkey In Me

I have a monkey in me
Climbing peacefully
Screeching viciously
Jumping happily
Swinging joyfully

Everybody notices her
Everybody likes her
She is a very happy monkey.

Kelly McIntosh (9)
Paradykes Primary School

I Have A Cat In Me

I have a cat in me
Sneaking quietly
Joyfully eating
Peacefully sleeping
Purring softly
Everybody likes him
He feels happy.

Aaron McIntosh (9)
Paradykes Primary School

I Have A Dog In Me

Barking loudly
Happily running
Peacefully sleeping
Eating hungrily
It feels very happy
People know it very well.

Calum Gray (9)
Paradykes Primary School

I Have A Rabbit In Me

I have a rabbit in me
Jumping quietly
Peacefully eating
Happily sleeping
Drinking joyfully
Nobody knows her.
She doesn't care
Because she is down in her lair.

Danielle Watson (9)
Paradykes Primary School

I Have A Monkey In Me

Swinging joyfully
Loudly screaming
Quickly eating
Climbing excitedly
Everybody likes him
Everybody crowds him
He feels like a team.

Jamie Ralston (9)
Paradykes Primary School

I Have A Cat In Me

I have a cat in me
Prowling eagerly
Ferociously pouncing
Silently dreaming
Quickly eating
Everybody knows him
He feels safe.

Callum Buntin (9)
Paradykes Primary School

I Have A Monkey In Me

I have a monkey in me
Climbing joyfully
Jumping viciously
Quickly swinging
Happily flying
Everybody knows him
Everybody likes him
He is very happy.

Scott Stenhouse (9)
Paradykes Primary School

I Have A Mouse In Me

I have a mouse in me
Walking quietly
Peacefully playing
Happily eating
Joyfully nibbling
Nobody knows her
But she doesn't care
She is safe.

Sarah Walker (9)
Paradykes Primary School

I Have A Cat In Me

I have a cat in me
Scratching viciously
Happily pouncing
Peacefully sleeping
Stretching tiredly
Everybody wants to cuddle him
He feels happy.

Scott Montgomery (9)
Paradykes Primary School

I Have A Spider In Me

I have a spider in me
Climbing rapidly
Eats flies ferociously
Sneaking quietly
Spinning a web beautifully
It hides frightfully
Watching weirdly
Sleeping peacefully
Everyone wants to stamp on him.

Logan Hercus (9)
Paradykes Primary School

I Have A Hippo In Me

I have a hippo in me
Swimming happily
Peacefully eating
Loudly sleeping
Running viciously
He has lots of friends
Mostly everybody knows him
He feels very calm.

Daniel Cherrie (9)
Paradykes Primary School

I Have A Rabbit In Me

I have a rabbit in me
Sitting quietly
Happily sleeping
Silently munching
Hopping joyfully
People recognise her
People know her
She is calm.

Kirsty Macbeath (9)
Paradykes Primary School

The Cow's Mouth

Once I saw a cow on a magic carpet
flying like a beaver in a rocket.
It was drinking its milk and eating its cheese
and herding to the movies.
It was wearing sunglasses and setting fire to the carpet.
Suddenly there was a *bang, boom, whizz* and a *pop*
and it turned into a genie.
Suddenly knights, dragons, frogs and parrots
cowboys, pirates, witches, wizards, cats, owls,
rats, monsters and spiders appeared out of nowhere.
In a flash they disappeared into the cow's mouth.

Tom Brooke (8)
St Mary's RC Primary School, Edinburgh

The Flying Pigs

Once I saw a flying pig who was wearing a wig.
She was heading for the park.
Then her family came along
And they played flying piggy tiggy.
Then it was time to go home.
I made friends with them.

Sophie Lynn (9)
St Mary's RC Primary School, Edinburgh

My Brother

My brother is a monster
he bites me and nips me.
When he is angry he calls himself Nip Man
and he hurts me.
My brother is such a devil
he makes my mum shout, 'Stop that!'

Declan Logan (9)
St Mary's RC Primary School, Edinburgh

My Funny Friends And Family

My mum plays a drum which makes my dad mad.
My brother is such a bother, just like my blister sister!
I have a dozen cousins, five hundred aunts
And then there's my gran, she just loves this silly old pan
And Grandpa number 200 just loves the spa!
My five best friends, Stephanie, Bethany, Charlotte,
Scarlett and Natasha the crasher!
Then there's my teacher, em, well let's not talk about her!
Oh did I tell you about my uncle, he makes great crumble!
Then there's me, me, Flora Hughes,
I'm just a little monkey I am!

Flora Hughes (8)
St Mary's RC Primary School, Edinburgh

Pollution

Pollution, pollution is bad for health.
Pollution, pollution is bad for creatures,
Ducks, birds, fish and goats.
Everything gets killed by that horrible smoke
It comes out of factories and out of cars so put it away.
Now it's safe birds can fly and sway
So say bye to the smoke I hope.

Oliver Smith (8)
St Mary's RC Primary School, Edinburgh

My Class

My class, my class, a funny old thing,
With Miss Reville, the Devil
And Nutty Natasha, Daffodil Declan, Loud-Mouth Louis
And Confusing Callum, Jammy Jordan, Sarcastic Sandy
And Gangster Garrett, Elastic Alicia.

My friends, my friends, so cool, so clean
With Famous Flora and Starfish Stephanie
Bamboo Bella and Physical Phoebe
Magic Marisha and Terrific Tallulah
Sometimes I think I'm the only normal one
And it drives me round the bend.

Charlotte Lazarowicz (8)
St Mary's RC Primary School, Edinburgh

Music

Music is magic, music is bright
as bright as a light.
Instruments make it sound so tragic.
All the sounds are there to learn
just pick up a pen and a song
for the show next week.
You'll start with a lah and then a fah
then add some instruments too.
Make it sound better
for you'll be the star of the show.

Marisha Worsnop (8)
St Mary's RC Primary School, Edinburgh

Music

I know a girl who can play the keyboard
Plinky, plonky, plinky, plonky.

I know a friend who can play the flute
Toot, toot, toot.

I know a boy who can play the tambourine
Jingle, jingle, jingle.

I know a man who can play the kazoo
Zoo, zoo, zoo.

I know a lady who can play the maraca
Shake, shake, shake.

Sometimes they all come together
To make a song that sounds like this.
Plinky, plonky, plinky, plonky, toot, toot, toot,
Jingle, jingle, jingle, zoo, zoo, zoo, shake, shake, shake.

Every afternoon they make a new tune.

Stephanie McAdam (8)
St Mary's RC Primary School, Edinburgh

Wildlife

Once I went to North Fife to try to explore the wildlife,
when I was halfway there I banged into the most fuzzy, scary bear.
His teeth were stuck together with yellow melting honey.
I took a step forward, I saw the world champion biggest bunny.
It had a pompom tail, I ran further in, I stood on a pin.
What a pin, I was about to go mentally insane.
I went to my granny's to have a cup of tea,
Then I went to have a quick pee.
I had seen everything and that was that
So then I went back to my Edinburgh flat.

Tallulah McCowan Hill (8)
St Mary's RC Primary School, Edinburgh

Don't Bully Me

Don't bully me, it makes me sad
Don't bully me, it drives me mad
Don't bully me, it is so bad
Don't bully me, I won't be glad

Don't hurt me, it makes me sad
Don't hurt me, it drives me mad
Don't hurt me, it is so bad
Don't hurt me, I won't be glad

Don't anger me, it makes me sad
Don't anger me, it drives me mad
Don't anger me, it is so bad
Don't anger me, I won't be glad

Don't abuse me, it makes me sad
Don't abuse me, it drives me mad
Don't abuse me, it is so bad
Don't abuse me, I won't be glad.

Lloyd Anderson (12)
St Peter's Primary School, Edinburgh

My Sadness

The colour of my sadness is white like a big lonely space.
My sadness smells like mud off the ground.
My sadness tastes like garbage crumbs.
My sadness sounds like screaming voices.
My sadness looks like a screaming child.
My sadness reminds me of non-stop pain.
My sadness feels like breaking bones.

Cameron Pullar (11)
St Peter's Primary School, Edinburgh

The Bullies

I am so scared.
I am so small.
I don't want to tell.
No not at all.

Horrible bullies.
All big and tough.
Hurting me loads.
They are in quite a big huff.

Then they take my snack
And I start crying.
From behind a bush
My best friend is spying.

Then I tell
And my mum is astonished.
The bullying then stops
And I am glad it has finished.

Stephanie Cremona (8)
St Peter's Primary School, Edinburgh

Bullying Has To Stop

The tears in my eyes
I stood there and cried
The bullies stood there and laughed
I cried and cried and tried to stop myself
But I just couldn't do it.
I told them to stop
But they just laughed.
I said, 'Please, please stop,'
But they just wouldn't.

Saoirse Robertson (9)
St Peter's Primary School, Edinburgh

Don't Bully

It isn't cool when you go to school
to hurt other children,
it makes you a fool!

Please be nice and join my fun,
share my snack and be my chum.

So don't kick or hit or pull my hair,
if you need a friend just say and I'll be there!

When you grow up you will think it's silly
to have spent all your childhood
being a bully.

So don't be a bully in the end
join in the fun and be my friend.

Lucy Malloy (8)
St Peter's Primary School, Edinburgh

Don't

Don't, don't, don't do that!
Don't tell Lauren Service she is nervous.
Don't tell Kim to sing a hymn.
Don't say to Claire she has fuzzy hair.

Don't, don't, don't do that!
Don't ask Chris to give a kiss.
Don't ask Joanna to eat a banana.
Don't tell Mrs Blair she's a grizzly bear.

Don't, don't, don't do that!
Don't say to Mrs Lilley she's very silly.
Don't tell Ellie she has a jelly belly.
Don't tell Ruth she never tells the truth.

Adele Pacitti (7)
St Peter's Primary School, Edinburgh

Bullied

Bullies always crowd around me,
Tell me what to do,
I always wonder,
Why can't you?

But I dare not say,
Otherwise I'll have to pay,
All of my lunch money
For today.

I run home
And cry on my pillow,
I'm being such a
Weeping willow.

The next day at school,
I go to the pool,
Where teachers are not watching
His arms are launching.

The next day
Lining up in a row,
I have the courage
To just say,

No!

Sam Jefferson (8)
St Peter's Primary School, Edinburgh

Fear

The colour of my fear is blue like dripping tears.
My fear smells like the coldness of outside.
My fear tastes like freezing ice.
My fear sounds like the gush of flowing water.
My fear looks like the sky with nothing in sight.
My fear reminds me of loneliness inside me.
My fear feels like nothing can see me.

Sarah Denholm (11)
St Peter's Primary School, Edinburgh

The Girl And The Bully

There the girl stood,
Battered well and truly,
There stood the bully,
Looking sly and unruly.

There stood her friend,
Peeking from a hideout,
There stood the bully's friend,
Starting to shout.

Why am I here?
Doing nothing at all,
Just because of my fear,
That I might fall.

I shall go,
Overcome my fear,
I shall be high not low,
Fearless and brave.

I went up to them,
Told them that it wasn't right,
They ran away,
I had won the fight!

Niamh Jarvis (8)
St Peter's Primary School, Edinburgh

Bullying

I hate bullying.
How about you?
If bullying was to stop
It would make life easier
For everyone in the world.
There would be no more tears
There would be no more unkindness
Wouldn't that make everyone feel better?

Shaun Newman (11)
St Peter's Primary School, Edinburgh

Bullies

Horrible bullies everywhere
Hitting and punching all the time
They don't even realise that they're hurting people.
People are getting annoyed.

I went to the bullies and said to them,
'How would you feel if you were bullied like them?'
The bullies said, 'So what, who cares?'
'I care, they care, the teachers care as well.'

The bullies said nothing
As I went to tell the teacher
Just as I went up, the bullies stopped me
And I thought, *yes!*

Lucie Keenan (8)
St Peter's Primary School, Edinburgh

A Person That Bullies Might Feel Sad

The colour of my sadness is blue like a painful bruise.
My sadness smells like someone's old, sweaty shoes.
My sadness tastes like rotten food that's out of date.
My sadness sounds like someone's wail when I kick them
on the train.
My sadness looks like a never-ending lane when I'm soaked
with the pouring rain.
My sadness reminds me of the look of pain on my victim's face.
My sadness feels like the tears that slowly trickle down my face . . .
Then disappear without a trace.

Eithne FitzGerald (11)
St Peter's Primary School, Edinburgh

Don't

Don't, don't, don't do that!
Don't eat Joanna instead of a banana.
Don't tell Claire, she looks like a bear.
Don't put Andrew into a pot of stew.

Don't, don't, don't do that!
Don't throw Adele in the wishing well.
Don't put Frank in the fish tank.
Don't tell Lauren Service she is nervous.

Don't, don't, don't do that!
Don't tell Ciara she hasn't got a tiara.
Don't let Emily Harkin do my marking.
Don't let Alice go to the palace.

Joanna Thomson (7)
St Peter's Primary School, Edinburgh

Don't

Don't, don't, don't do that!
Don't say Kiara has a tiny tiara.
Don't say Dave isn't very brave!
Don't tell Sam he looks like ham!

Don't, don't, don't do that!
Don't say Ben looks like a hen.
Don't tell Frank his ship has sank.
Don't go and tell Tony he looks like a pony.

Don't, don't, don't do that!
Don't put Alice in a palace.
Don't tell Ross he is the boss.
Don't tell Chris to give you a kiss.

Ciara Sawey (7)
St Peter's Primary School, Edinburgh

Get The World Anti-Bully

If someone pulled your hair, what would it be like?
If someone called you a bad name, what would it be like?
If someone excluded you, what would it be like?
If someone were unkind to you, what would it be like?

Bully is like a big brown bear,
they could growl at you at any time, anywhere.
Bully is as scary as it could be,
like a shark ready to bite you in the sea.
Bully could make you cry your head off,
so become anti-bully now!

Use a heart full of love,
a friendship with kindness,
a big soap to wash off every single bully,
so make the world become anti-bully now.

Lishan Qian (9)
St Peter's Primary School, Edinburgh

Bullying

Why am I being bullied?
Why do these people tease me?
What have I done wrong?
I really don't understand.

I hate it, in fact I detest it
I am unhappy, in fact I am very unhappy.
The bully is always waiting for me.

Take me anywhere
But nowhere near the bully
I am sick and tired of it.

I don't know what you think
But no one's as bad as the bully.

Beth Howard (9)
St Peter's Primary School, Edinburgh

The Bully And Me

I don't like the bully!
I don't feel safe
I feel really shy
And he looks sly

He is so mean
He is so scary
He makes me feel
Just so sad

I have a hiding place
So I can hide
He knows where it is
So he waits 'til I come out

My hiding place is so cool
But the problem is
He is always there.

Martina Rossi (9)
St Peter's Primary School, Edinburgh

A Recipe For An Anti-Bullying Cake

First you need to get a pinch of hope.
Wash your racist hands with non-bullying soap.
Add a pinch of joy.
Add 2 teaspoons of niceness to give it spice.

Add a cup of friendship,
A mug of love,
A sprinkle of peace,
Add a slice of sweetness.

Add a spoon of truth.
Don't lose your tooth when you eat it.
Make sure you enjoy it.
That's how to make a non-bullying cake.

Francesca Faichney (9)
St Peter's Primary School, Edinburgh

Room For Racism

Here I stand in this room
Surrounded by people of different coloured skin
I feel nervous and worried
They all start calling me names
And I feel surprised and lonely
All of them seem to have a friend except me
I feel unpopular when they call me names
I feel stupid and small and powerless
When they push me I feel frightened and sad
I also feel angry at them for doing this to me
When I notice an old friend I feel puzzled
And ask her why she is doing this
She answers me in a very strange way,
'Because I am scared,' she says
And I can see the fear in her eyes.

Emily Turnbull (8)
St Peter's Primary School, Edinburgh

The Bullies

Bullies hide other people's things.
Sometimes even steal them.
Bullies are evil.
Never go near them.
They could beat you up any time
Or do something else.
Never be beaten by the bullies.
Keep yourself safe.

Lewis Gormley (8)
St Peter's Primary School, Edinburgh

Loneliness

My loneliness is grey like a rain cloud,
hanging in the sky.
My loneliness smells like an unknown scent,
strange in your nose.
My loneliness tastes like hard, stale bread,
too dry to be eaten.
My loneliness sounds like a sad, sad song,
played on a violin.
My loneliness looks like an abandoned baby,
pathetic and helpless.
My loneliness reminds me of an empty house,
unlived in for years.
My loneliness feels like an everlasting hunger,
painful and unending.

Moreen Randall (11)
St Peter's Primary School, Edinburgh

Powerful

The colour of my power is dark blue like a stormy sea.
My power smells like burning diesel.
My power tastes like spicy chillis.
My power sounds like a thundering waterfall.
My power looks like angry lightning.
My power reminds me of a very strong bear.
My power feels like carrying a heavy weight.

Leon Siebke Ballin (11)
St Peter's Primary School, Edinburgh

A Victim Of Bullying

I am a victim of bullying,
It makes me very sad,
I am a victim of bullying,
It makes every school day bad.

I am a victim of bullying,
I play all on my own,
I am a victim of bullying,
It makes me feel alone.

I am a victim of bullying,
It makes me feel depressed,
I am a victim of bullying,
I never get any rest.

I am a victim of bullying,
I haven't let anyone know,
I am a victim of bullying,
I wish they'd just let go!

Ronan Mullan (11)
St Peter's Primary School, Edinburgh

Bullies

Bullies are bad, bullies break your bones
Bullies are nasty, they're not kind
They steal phones and put them in other people's bags
They get into trouble and think that's a laugh
They tease and push people and give them a hard time
They wind people up to get them all annoyed
They hurt other's feelings and don't really care
They poke and punch people and say it was not them
Bullies are a pest and think they are the best
But we know life's better without them.

James Monan (8)
St Peter's Primary School, Edinburgh

Bully

All of the school were mean to me,
Only because I hurt my knee,
When I was in a lot of pain
I had only a little strain
For I was very upset.

The next day I came to my school,
I wanted to play in the pool,
All they said was 'go away'!
When I only said, 'Can I play?'
For I was very upset.

When I was not feeling great
And when I was turning eight
They said 'Happy birthday'.
After that it all stopped,
Yes, the whole lot.

Sophie Darbyshire (10)
St Peter's Primary School, Edinburgh

Bullies Are Evil

Bullies are bad,
Bullies are horrible,
So if you see a bully bullying other kids,
Tell the teacher and they will sort it out,
And make others happy.

Cathy Chiduku (8)
St Peter's Primary School, Edinburgh

Susan Walker

Oh no, she is coming,
Susan Walker, the bully,
Here she comes,
With her gang of girls.
She is coming to bully me.

'Hey, flat face,' she says,
Spitting on me,
And grabbing me as I try to run past,
'Oh,' she says, 'why go so soon, black girl?'
I feel embarrassed and hurt,
I shiver and then I shout.

'Just because I'm black, why bully me?
Why pick on me, just because I'm Indian?
I'm different, so what, I'm proud of who I am,'
And then I stand there watching her,
She is crying.

I run home rejoicing for I have defeated the bully,
I am happy now, I am smiling,
I will make friends with the bully
And we will have fun together,
I smile.

Chloe Bruce-Gardyne (10)
St Peter's Primary School, Edinburgh

Happiness

Happiness is like the blazing yellow sun.
Happiness looks like clear blue running water.
Happiness tastes like a big birthday cake.
Happiness sounds like children laughing.
Happiness smells like fresh-cut grass.
Happiness feels like someone telling you it's really good.
It is like a bouncing ball on the beach
With children running to catch it.
It's like when you finish a race filled with pride.

Rose Johnstone (11)
St Peter's Primary School, Edinburgh

The Terrible School

I hate my school, they call me names
They won't let me join in their games
It's because I'm what they call a foreigner
They push me hard into a corner.

They are passing notes about my race
Outside they kick me and spit on my face
They rip my emerald clothes apart
I feel so sad, it breaks my heart.

They text me threats
I try to forget
But I can't 'cause it's tough
I'm really angry, I've had enough.

I'm marching up to Mrs Hoolie
To tell her all about the bully
Mrs Hoolie and I talked and talked
After that the bullying stopped.

Anna McNairney (10)
St Peter's Primary School, Edinburgh

At School

At school I am bullied
Because I'm white.
I've been living
In China for two years now
And not told anybody
About the bullies.
Yet now I think I really should tell,
So I've told and now it's stopped
And I am entering
The world of happiness
And I have lots of friends.
Now I can call my school safe.

Sophie McKenzie (10)
St Peter's Primary School, Edinburgh

My Exotic Paradise

I lived in an exotic paradise,
I was happy where it was hot,
How the days were long,
The nights were short,
But that has all changed now.

I knew it was different,
As soon as I stepped off the plane,
It was cold and dark,
It was the Scottish winter,
I knew.

At school I was pushed against the wall,
Called names like 'Flat Face' and 'Brownie',
When I got home my hair was a mess,
I really cannot tell my mum.

Day after day, night after night,
They teased me and hurt me,
I felt so sad,
At night I cried so no one would hear,
The tears ran down my face,
As I cuddled up under the duvet.

I'm happy now,
As I sit in my exotic paradise,
No bullies, no racists,
I am happy where it is hot.

Erin Mackinnon (10)
St Peter's Primary School, Edinburgh

Going Back

I have just moved from India
I thought it would be fine
Until I met them
The bullies.

They corner me at break
Shouting racist comments
About my skin tone
And my different religion
Now they're using physical violence
I don't know what's worse
If I tell they threaten to kill me!

Then I think about it
If I tell then that person
Will protect me.

I finally pluck up enough courage
I tell my mum
She understands
We're going back
To where I belong.

Lisa Wilson (10)
St Peter's Primary School, Edinburgh

Autumn

A utumn is a colourful month with red and gold.
U p and down go the birds picking red berries.
T he trees' leaves fall off the trees in autumn.
U p go umbrellas when the rainy weather starts.
M aking funny masks for Hallowe'en.
N ature is gold in autumn.

Tom Donovan (7)
St Peter's Primary School, Edinburgh

Jealousy

Jealousy is like a big piece of green mould
which has been lying around for days.

Jealousy sounds like lots of people
speaking about all their new stuff that no one else has.

Jealousy tastes like my gran's disgusting boiled cabbage
that we have on Christmas Day.

Jealousy smells like a huge pile of horse dung
that has been sitting there for one week.

Jealousy looks like a collection
of big, shiny gold medals.

Jealousy feels like lying in a big bed
of slimy mushy peas.

Jealousy reminds me of the time I got a game
and my sister got an iPod.

Patrick Faichney (11)
St Peter's Primary School, Edinburgh

Love

Love is pink like a piece of beautiful spring blossom,
travelling through a cool breeze.
It sounds like a fresh morning with birds singing in the trees.
It tastes like a nice warm bowl of chicken soup.
It smells like a big bowl of the finest chocolate
melted into a yummy mixture.
It looks like a newly picked rose from the nearest garden.
It feels like a gorgeous sunny day by the seashore,
with the sand between my toes and the water down below.
Love reminds me of a crisp, fast-flowing stream
that leads to a large, beautiful lake.

Kirsty Galbraith (10)
St Peter's Primary School, Edinburgh

Sadness

Sadness is blue
like being at a funeral
with nobody else there.
Sadness sounds like lots of people crying.
Sadness tastes like a horrible watermelon.
It smells like a dead body
in a coffin gently laid down
in a church on a very dull night.
Sadness looks like a poor old woman
at home all alone with nobody
to talk to and nothing to do.
It feels like nobody letting you join in,
in games that you enjoy.
Sadness reminds me of five years ago
when my dad died.

Sarah O'Brien (11)
St Peter's Primary School, Edinburgh

Don't

Don't, don't, don't do that!
Don't put a bear on Tony Blair
Don't put ants in my dad's pants
Don't call Simon a big lion.

Don't, don't, don't do that!
Don't call Anna a banana
Don't twist Mrs Scott in a knot
Don't tell Sean he's a yummy scone.

Don't, don't, don't do that!
Don't put the cat in Grandpa's hat
Don't tell Grandma she's my grandpa
Don't tell Tom he's a bomb.

Simon Wilson (7)
St Peter's Primary School, Edinburgh

Hatred

Hatred is red like an exploding volcano
with lava pouring down its sides, destroying every house it touches.
Hatred sounds like a million scratching chalkboards
and howling dogs at their loudest.
Hatred tastes like worms and maggots coming out of your mouth.
Hatred smells like a bucketful of sick left there all week.
Hatred looks like a snarling queue of people
trying to get their money on payday.
Hatred feels like jagged thorns digging into your palms.
Hatred reminds me of someone being sick,
then I want to be sick too!

Nicole Ojok (11)
St Peter's Primary School, Edinburgh

Jealousy

Jealousy is green like a fierce green dragon blowing hot flames.
It sounds like a train going full speed past you.
Jealousy tastes like sand in your sandwiches,
                         a gritty mess in-between your teeth.
It smells like a smashed raw egg after lying outside for a few days.
Jealousy looks like a 1st prize trophy on someone else's shelf.
It feels like a hairy tarantula crawling slowly over your hand.
Jealousy reminds me of a girl sitting on her own with a bully
                                                teasing her.

Lucy Cairns (11)
St Peter's Primary School, Edinburgh

Craziness

Craziness is yellow like a happy hyper kid in the hot sun.
It sounds like a clown in a circus telling funny jokes.
It tastes like a raw yellow pepper waiting to be cooked.
Craziness smells like fresh air when you're tumbling about.
It looks like doing a silly dance while having a laugh with friends.
It feels like you're doing an insane cartwheel and you fall.
Craziness will remind you of that berserk day
when you were running round the garden screaming, 'La la la la la!'
Craziness isn't black like a horrible old leopard climbing a tree.
Craziness is yellow and it is the best.

Fraser Johnston (11)
St Peter's Primary School, Edinburgh

Fear

Fear is black, like being closed into a deep, long darkness.
It tastes like cobwebs slowly melting to dust in your mouth.
It smells like one thousand years of bad breath, continuing to rot.
It sounds like a loud scream in the distance, giving you
                                        an unbearable headache.
It looks like a ghostly silhouette sending shivers up your spine.
It feels like maggots gnawing away at your nerves.
Fear reminds me of a cold morning, crisp and untouched.

Carrie Malloy (11)
St Peter's Primary School, Edinburgh

Bullying

If I was a bully I would hit, punch and kick,
Never ever being nice except to my friends,
If you weren't my friend, I would kick, punch, nip and munch,
In a vicious way.

A bully would treat me like a dog,
All they'd ever do is call me a snob
And cry baby,
Don't become a bully.

Never be a bully if you want some friends,
Just make the world anti-bullying,
Do you want to be mean all the time, everywhere?
Just don't become a bully, please!

Rhona Lilley (9)
St Peter's Primary School, Edinburgh

Big Bad Bullies

Big bad bullies, evil as ever.
Big bad bullies, nasty as hell.
Big bad bullies, racist and sexist.
Big bad bullies, stealing your trust.
Big bad bullies, annoying and upsetting.
Big bad bullies, really stupid.
Big bad bullies, forever and ever.

Marc Fleming (9)
St Peter's Primary School, Edinburgh

The Bully

The bully walks down the path,
Then all the noise stops,
The racers stop, everything stops!

The bully picks whom to attack,
He picks Len then he starts to attack,
Black guy! Idiot! Fatty pig!

I'm running to an adult for help,
I'm running as fast as a fox,
But the bully throws a rock!

The bully walks into the office,
The bully is scared as the head says,
'Boris you naughty boy!'

Andrei Vitaliev (9)
St Peter's Primary School, Edinburgh

If . . .

If I were a bully what would it be like?
Hurting someone or stealing a bike
It wouldn't be kind.

If I was being bullied it would be terrifying.
I might be quite nasty to people
Because of my feelings.

To stop it might seem difficult
But it really must be done.
Together we can stop them.
Let's go tell someone!

Finlay MacKenzie (9)
St Peter's Primary School, Edinburgh

Fear

It is black like the bringers of doom,
It sounds like the rumble of distant thunder,
It tastes like your insides in your mouth,
It smells like the filthy stench of vomit,
It looks like the darkest shadow from the deepest pits of Hell,
It feels like a thundercloud filled with hate,
It reminds me of darkness that can only be evil.

What is it? *Fear!*

It seems like the worst possible thing on Earth,
It is darkness, evil and sadness all in one,
It travels through people like contagious diseases,
It moves like lightning gaining power,
It takes control over everything.

What is it? *Fear!*

Nothing can stop it except one thing,
But against all others it moves without stopping.

What is it? *Fear!*

Aidan Mooney (11)
St Peter's Primary School, Edinburgh

Love

Love is pink, like a sweet-smelling cherry tree in full bloom.
It sounds like birdsong on a bright summer's morning.
It tastes like cream cakes fresh from the oven.
It smells like a marshmallow, very soft to touch.
It looks like a colourful rainbow in the sky above me.
It reminds me of my rosy-cheeked cousin
                laughing at me as I play with her.

Kirsty Lilley (11)
St Peter's Primary School, Edinburgh

Love

Love is the colour pink like a pink rose,
newly bloomed in summer.

Love sounds like a harp,
played gently and gracefully by angels.

It tastes like chocolate,
made with love and care and tastes so sweet.

It smells like a newly made loaf,
too hot to eat but smells delicious.

Love looks like a swan,
gracefully floating along the river.

Love feels like a warm summer's day
when you're relaxing on the beach.

It reminds me of my family,
caring always and keeping a smile on my face.

This is how I would describe love.

Katie Jefferson (11)
St Peter's Primary School, Edinburgh

Bullies

Bullies aren't good,
Bullies aren't smart,
They may steal someone's phone,
Or break someone's bones,
But they must feel very alone.

Jacqueline Flynn (8)
St Peter's Primary School, Edinburgh

Jealousy

Jealousy is green like the green eyes of a cat,
ready to pounce onto a mouse.

It tastes like the poisonous graveyard gravel,
grotesquely rotting away in my mouth.

It sounds like a grenade,
exploding on the grassy meadows.

It smells like the rotting apples on the tree,
growing out of control.

It looks like a terrible storm,
loud and horrible.

It feels like the wind,
cold and about to blow you away.

It reminds me of a field,
green and silent.

Silvie Walker (11)
St Peter's Primary School, Edinburgh

Jealousy

Jealousy, jealousy is green,
like a cat's eyes in the dark.

Jealousy, jealousy looks like a light mist,
spreading everywhere, unable to stop.

Jealousy, jealousy tastes like lime liquorice,
disgusting and strong.

Jealousy, jealousy smells like a stuffy room
where you can hardly breathe.

Jealousy, jealousy feels like a rash all over your face,
that no product can calm.

Jealousy, jealousy reminds me of a cold winter's day,
unwelcome and unfriendly.

Lucy Sharpe (11)
St Peter's Primary School, Edinburgh

Fear

Fear is black, like a dark, scary alleyway.

It sounds like shouts and screams of children
as bullies look down and threaten them with their big tough faces.

Fear tastes like stale, lumpy, mushy porridge
and it smells like manure when it's being spread on the fields.

Fear looks like shadows of who knows what
lurking deep down in the basement of your house.

Fear feels like voices in your head telling you to run
but your feet are stuck to the ground.

It reminds you of the dentist
as he drills through your teeth
shining a blinding light into your eyes.

Catherine Donovan (11)
St Peter's Primary School, Edinburgh

Being Bullied

My face all bruised and battered
My heart feels like it's shattered
As I fall to the ground
I can hear a dreadful sound
'Ha ha ha,' everyone shouts
But I still have my doubts
I stand up and fight back
But I just can't keep track
He hits me in the face
And I choke on my brace
I walk away but stumble
Until I hear a mumble
I scream, shout and also yell,
'I hope you go to Hell.'

Molly McCloy (11)
St Peter's Primary School, Edinburgh

I'd Like To Show You The Door

Racism stomps in,
Slamming the door behind,
Angry look on its face,
Staring out of big, red, fierce eyes,
Terrifying voice shouting out.

I stand up and in a gentle, friendly voice,
I say, 'I'd like to show you the door.'

Amy O'Sullivan-Robertson (8)
St Peter's Primary School, Edinburgh

Racism

Racism is black
Like a dark hole that never ends.
It tastes like bitter medicine.
It smells like blue Stilton.
It feels like one hundred spears cornering you.
This is how the victim felt.
How would you feel?

Sarah Wilson (8)
St Peter's Primary School, Edinburgh

Scared!

Being bullied is like a dark, dark cave that never ends,
And feels like a million swords surrounding you,
It smells like old dustbins.

Bullying is bad, it makes me feel sad!

Ciara Keenan (8)
St Peter's Primary School, Edinburgh

Bullies

B ullies are mean, they want to control and hurt you.
U nhappiness is the result of being bullied.
L ots of people know that bullies are selfish.
L ots of people get bullied and
I t makes them feel small, sad and alone.
E veryone wants a peaceful, happy world.
S o if you are a bully, quit now!

Flora Bruce-Gardyne (8)
St Peter's Primary School, Edinburgh

My Boots

My boots, my boots,
they're too little for me.
Please help me put them on!
My mum says, 'Take them back to the shop,'
but I say, 'No, no, no!'

I love these boots
but the problem is they're just too little for me,
but I won't take them back,
no, no, no, no,
these boots belong to me!

Skye Sutherland (9)
Stoneyburn Primary School

Silence

Silence is white like the cold winter snow
It reminds me of playing with my friends in the snow
It looks like the clouds up above
It tastes like water in your mouth
It sounds like people crunching through the snow
It smells like fresh milk out of a cow
Silence feels like a soft marshmallow.

James Bleakley (10)
Stoneyburn Primary School

Best Friends

If I'm upset my friends are always there,
because they really care.
If I fell down a drain
Skye would really complain.
If someone bullied me,
Kelsey would beat them up and say,
'Easy as 1, 2, 3!'
If I fell in a puddle
Niamh would give me a cuddle.
If I went in a huff
Shannon wouldn't act all gruff!
If I had to get a plaster,
Emma wouldn't say, 'Oh tttt, disaster!'
When I broke my finger
Kayleigh treated me like a famous singer.
If I bumped my head
Jasmine would send me straight to bed.
If a dog bit me on my leg
Katie would cheer me up by saying,
'It's a stinky egg!'

Francesca McGraw (9)
Stoneyburn Primary School

Shadows

Shadows walking round the room,
as scary as a bear walking behind you.
Then the shadows walk the other way,
like sharks looking for their prey.
Then a voice squeaks out
as quiet as a mouse.

Katie Abbott (9)
Stoneyburn Primary School

Sadness

Sadness is blue like the light blue sky.
Sadness looks like an old man, lonely on a bench.
Sadness smells like the open air.
Sadness sounds like my little sister crying.
It reminds me of a boring trip.
Sadness tastes like fresh water just out of a tap.

Jamie Green (9)
Stoneyburn Primary School

Best Friends

Best friends tell you secrets,
Best friends always play,
Best friends send you postcards
When they go away!

Summar Blair (9)
Stoneyburn Primary School